Pssst... It Worked!

JODIE BAUDEK

BALBOA.
PRESS

A DIVISION OF HAY HOUSE

Balboa Press books may be ordered through booksellers or by contacting:

Balboa Press
A Division of Hay House
1663 Liberty Drive
Bloomington, IN 47403
www.balboapress.com
1 (877) 407-4847

Because of the dynamic nature of the Internet, any web addresses or links contained in this book may have changed since publication and may no longer be valid. The views expressed in this work are solely those of the author and do not necessarily reflect the views of the publisher, and the publisher hereby disclaims any responsibility for them.

The author of this book does not dispense medical advice or prescribe the use of any technique as a form of treatment for physical, emotional, or medical problems without the advice of a physician, either directly or indirectly. The intent of the author is only to offer information of a general nature to help you in your quest for emotional and spiritual well-being. In the event you use any of the information in this book for yourself, which is your constitutional right, the author and the publisher assume no responsibility for your actions.

Any people depicted in stock imagery provided by Thinkstock are models, and such images are being used for illustrative purposes only. Certain stock imagery © Thinkstock.

Print information available on the last page.

ISBN: 978-1-5043-8233-5 (sc)
ISBN: 978-1-5043-8234-2 (e)

Library of Congress Control Number: 2017909415

Balboa Press rev. date: 10/11/2017

CONTENTS

The Challenge

As human beings, we've got kind of a big problem. We're not very nice to ourselves and we don't even realize it.

We look in the mirror and complain about what we see there. Then we look in our bank accounts and complain about what we see (or don't see) there. We compare ourselves to others, thinking we are unworthy of what they have, and always seem to come up as "less than" – our clothes aren't right, our hair isn't right, we're too old, we're too fat, we don't have enough money, education, or *enough of anything* to satisfy our worst critics. This leads to us feeling like *we are not enough* as a whole.

We usually imagine those critics as outside ourselves — our family members, bosses, co-workers, people we encounter in our daily lives — but **the heartbreaking reality is that often the worst criticisms come from *ourselves*, from that voice inside our heads that constantly tells us we don't measure up.**

When I talk to my clients about the thoughts that run

through their heads many times a day, they report things like this:

> *You never do anything right.*
> *You're not good enough.*
> *No wonder no one loves you.*
> *You're such a screw up.*
> *How could you be so naive?*
> *You're such a failure.*
> *Everyone thinks you're a loser.*
> *You could have done so much better.*

Be honest now, would we ever, *ever* talk this way to someone? Most of us wouldn't even say these things to someone we detested, let alone someone we loved! How can we give ourselves less of a break than we'd give our worst enemy?

Although it's impossible to know the exact number, it's estimated that we have between 12,000 and 60,000 conscious thoughts a day, with millions more bits of information passing through our brains unconsciously every second. Of these thoughts, it's estimated that 70-80% of them are negative, and most of them are exactly the same as the thoughts we had the day before.

That's a lot of negativity and repetition. It's no wonder these thoughts become "facts" to us after years of saying them over and over, and we often get used to feeling bad about ourselves. It's so familiar that it becomes comfortable in a strange way. Believe it or not, for a lot of people, being happy can actually be a scary thing to imagine! People become so complacent where they are in their emotions, that happiness just seems foreign to them. Well my friend, I want you to get comfortable being uncomfortable! It is time for change!

One of the biggest problems with all this negativity is that it's contagious, it spreads. When you tear yourself down constantly, you're creating a lens through which you view the entire world. Since every judgment is a reflection of how you're feeling about yourself, you're that much more likely to tear somebody else down, even when you don't want to. Your negative reaction to someone confirms for them all the negative things they're thinking about themselves — and it ripples out from there. Imagine whole groups of people *unconsciously* interacting with one another, guided by their own worst fears about themselves — well, you can see how it can get messy in a hurry. No wonder the lady at the post office snapped at you and that guy cut you off on the freeway. All that negativity can make the world a very grumpy, very unhappy place.

If we look at it from the standpoint of how the brain works, we can see that repetition = habit. Our negative thoughts are a habit. The great news is, that like any habit, this one can be replaced with something healthy and life-giving.

How?

It comes down to the simple, but not necessarily easy task, of training ourselves to react and talk to ourselves the way we would react and talk to someone we love more than anything in the world. **Can you imagine being for yourself what you are for your kids, your partner, your beloved pets, your closest friends?**

It might seem impossible, but I want to tell you the truth, **I know what a huge difference a little self-love can make.** I've seen it happen time after time – when people learn how to love themselves, they actually pay it forward. They smile at that lady at the post office, so maybe she smiles at the next customer in line. They don't get mad at the guy who cut them off on the road, because for all you know that person could have been rushing to the hospital and didn't even recognize he was upsetting them. Amazing things happen when you feel too good to dwell on the negative.

So it got me thinking…

If I could find a way to build more people up and help them to love themselves, could I actually be part of making the world a better place?

I wanted to find out.

So I put together a little experiment. Well, actually it was a book — a little book with simple actions to take every day for 31 days. I called it *Pssst - Wanna Get Out of Your Own Way?*, and I filled it with one month of specific things to do each day that would help people feel good about themselves and find the joy in life, as opposed to being complacent and wondering if this is all that I am.

All kinds of people bought the book and accepted the challenge — mostly people in my own hometown, which you'll hear a little bit about in a minute, but also people around the world who were looking for something, anything, to help them change their perspective.

I'm happy, excited and honored to say, the experiment worked!

Over the next hundred or so pages you'll find out how

and why. You'll meet some of the people who participated in the experiment and hear their stories, in their own words, of exactly how a little bit of self-love has changed their lives for the better.

This book is about more than sharing the results of my little experiment. My hope is that, inside these pages, you'll find the inspiration you need to make the changes that will make *your* own life better. Along with their stories and the unique ways they took on this challenge, you'll get insights into what opens up the possibility of radical transformation, even in the darkest times, and you'll come away with some practical ways to help you retrain your brain to make that happen.

Honestly – isn't it time you realized what an amazing, awesome human being you are?

If you're not quite sure how to answer that question, I'll answer it for you, YES. The time is now.

So stick with me. I'm here to help show you how.

CHAPTER 1

**So this strange woman in a book just told you
she's going to help you fall in love with yourself...**

And you may be wondering...who in the world is this woman and why is she so sure she can help me? What does she even know about me anyway?

Good question. Or questions.

My name is Jodie Baudek, and most people know me as a yoga teacher, but there's more to it than just that.

First off, I'm not one of those "Ohhhhmmmmmmm, I do yoga" people who thinks she has all the answers. My life is as dusty and real as the next person's, I swear! In fact, *I do swear* – but my work with yoga, meditation, and teaching has also brought a peace and kindness into my world that wasn't always there. I enjoy my occasional martinis and wine, but I've made the choice to eat natural foods. I love rock and roll, and I've been known to bust a move, even during yoga class! I love to be silly and spontaneous.

In other words, I am a normal person. Sort of.

I live and work in Shorewood, Illinois, a small, suburban town about 45 minutes south of Chicago. It's the area that was made famous in the movie *The Blues Brothers*, if you were around in the '80s.

Shorewood doesn't take up a lot of space on the map. It takes only 15 minutes to drive from one end of town to the other. However, within those 15 minutes, you will experience all kinds of people, from all across the social spectrum.

Blue collar workers, middle class professionals and millionaires all live together, in pretty much perfect harmony. You go to the local grocery store and everyone knows each other — that's just how it is in small towns!

Shorewood is also the type of place where most people never leave. They grow up here, get married, have kids, go to work, and repeat, repeat, repeat — every single day, year after year after year. In other words, it's like a lot of towns all across America.

Maybe even yours.

Opening a yoga studio in a town like Shorewood was kind of a challenge. This is not like a lot of bigger cities, where there's a yoga studio on every corner. It's not like people here were begging for yoga classes. A lot of them see yoga as a little bit "woo-woo" — the sort of thing people out in L.A. do, like raw food cleanses and going vegan and energy healing. Most folks around here don't care all that much about reaching enlightenment, or nirvana, or any of that stuff. In fact, they don't spend a lot of time thinking about themselves at all. They think that's selfish. Besides, they've got too much stuff to do. There are bills to pay, kids to feed, houses to clean, and of course, there's always work, work, work.

If anything is going to get them into my studio, it's their health. These people work so hard, they forget to take care of themselves, until they reach the point where they need to get healthier and feel better. And since exercise is something people put in the "have to do" category, as opposed to the "want to do" category, they don't need to feel as guilty about making time to work out.

That's how I get them in the door.

Still, about a decade ago, when I first opened Essence of Life (the name of my studio), getting those people in *my* door, as opposed to the aerobics class down the street, wasn't easy. I had to do all kinds of crazy things just to get people to check me out. I was constantly re innovating my space and the extra filler classes - I stayed on top of the latest fitness trends! Don't get me wrong, they were all a blast, and people loved them.

But that's not my passion.

What I cared the most about, and what I wanted to share with the people of Shorewood, was yoga. I knew it would make a huge difference in their lives, just like it did for me and for so many others I've seen.

It was my mission.

I like to say that yoga is a front. It's a complete workout — you get everything you need from it from a physical standpoint. But there's so much more to it than that. Yoga engages your body, your mind and your spirit — all at the same time. It actually *does* connect you with your consciousness and helps you feel more peaceful, whether that sounds "woo-woo" to you or not!

The problem was, how was I going to sell inner peace to

people who think all that stuff is kind of b.s. that isn't really worth their time?

What I did was work hard to gain people's trust. No matter what the name of the class happened to be (yes, even boot camp!), underneath the surface, I would always sneak in a little bit of yoga. Whatever class you happened to show up for, you'd be doing a few yoga poses — I guarantee it!

My clients didn't complain. They liked it. It was catching on.

I also mixed up the yoga classes I offered. To keep people's interest, instead of playing the usual New-Agey, *ohmmmmm* type music in the background, I played dance music, or hip hop, or rock and roll — to appeal to all different kinds of people. If I made it fun for them, I knew they would keep coming back.

And they did. Shorewood, Illinois was doing yoga!

Eventually, the demand for yoga grew enough that I was able to retire some of the fitness classes and offer more of what I love. I'd tell my clients, "If you have to give up anything at all, any of your workouts, do not give up your yoga." Luckily, they listened to me. And like so many people who open the door just a crack and make yoga a part of their lives, they got to love it.

This was the perfect window of opportunity to deliver the type of classes I really wanted to — the kind that transform not only the body, but the mind and soul, as well.

For that one hour a day, my clients belong to me. And I want to make the time count.

So that mission I talked about earlier, where I want to build people up and teach them to love themselves, that work actually started in my yoga classes. It still goes on today. Of course we still sit in lotus position and do poses like warrior and tree and downward dog. But there's more to class.

At the end of every class, I ask everyone to join me in a 10-minute meditation. Then I ask them to answer these three questions:

> *What are you grateful for?*
> *What goals do you have?*
> *What do you like about yourself?*

Three basic questions. It sounds simple, right?
Wrong.

Those questions aren't always easy to answer – especially that last one! "What do I like about myself?" — you'd be amazed how difficult this is for people.

People joke about it — but at the root of it is something very real to them. "What do I like about myself?" It would be way easier to answer it if was, "*What **don't** you like about yourself?*"

I get a look of confusion — and sometimes fear. There's often a long pause as they rack their brains trying to come up with one tiny little answer, but they can't. Maybe after they ponder for a while, they'll finally come up with something basic, like "I'm nice" or "my smile."

But that's not my goal. I want them to dig deep and speak from their soul.

The thing is, over time, they actually change. And their responses change, too. The answers come more quickly and straight from the heart. Instead of mumbling, they're able to open up and shout out in confidence how kick ass they truly are!

That's the beauty of it, and why this is my mission in life. *With the right tools and practice, we can un-learn the habit of cutting ourselves down, and we can cultivate a new habit of loving ourselves.*

This is where I believe the real power of yoga comes through. I watch my clients become stronger — not only physically, but mentally and spiritually, too. Their outlook on themselves and life changes. And guess what? They actually do achieve the most important things: genuine happiness and (yes, it's true) inner peace!

That's why I put those three questions at the heart of the book I wrote and the experiment I developed. It's the thread that connected each of these amazing people on their journeys.

I'm so excited for you to meet them. They, like you, are strong, powerful, so beautiful, and are filled with limitless possibility.

Are you ready? It's time to dive in.

Chapter 2

*Throughout all of history, people have been
fascinated with feats of superhuman strength.
We're told tales of gods that move mountains
and men that wrestle lions with their bare hands.
But in truth, the most heroic acts of all are the
weights everyday people lift within themselves.*

—Beau Taplin, "Everyday Superman"

Marie, Age 47

Superpowers: Her love for others and her big, generous heart

What was in her way: Guilt and self-doubt

Day 1 Story: *I can have feelings, but I just can't say them out
loud. I often feel guilty when I ask for what I want or when
I try to set boundaries.*

Spend five minutes with Marie, and you'll notice a few
things. There's a regal quality to the way she carries
herself, a spark of confidence in her dark eyes, a glint of
mischief in her smile and her easy laugh. She holds a certain

kind of brightness, and you can feel it when you're around her. She's fierce and full of love.

Would it surprise you to know that one of her greatest challenges is finding the courage to trust and take care of herself? It's a struggle she's faced since she was a child — a story from an unstable childhood that stayed with her well into adulthood. Maybe you know what that feels like, too.

Before she started her 31-day journey, she struggled to say "yes" when she wanted to. She struggled to say "no" when she wanted to. And if she did, she felt guilty for days afterward, overanalyzing and re-hashing interactions and conversations in her head, wishing she could make everyone happy. The result? In an endless effort to make others happy, she rarely felt happiness herself. She didn't take restorative time for herself, and she often got sucked into cycles of drama and conflict in her personal and family relationships. Marie was tired, worn out, completely drained. She often felt weak in relationships and resented those who didn't respect her boundaries — even as she struggled to set limits.

"The book gave me a lot of courage. It held me accountable," she says, letting out a deep breath, like she's releasing something heavy inside. And she needed that courage. Going through the book, doing the work, and keeping the journal dug up a lot of unresolved issues — things she had to face, days and conversations that were uncomfortable, old habits that have caused her a great deal of suffering in recent years.

Marie's primary challenge was to start listening—really

listening—and learning to trust that guiding voice inside her that was urging her to take care of herself. She was good at ignoring it and at finding ways to tell herself that she didn't *really* need, or even deserve, that space for self-care. Getting out of her own way involved being super intentional about stilling that noisy inner critic, calming the child inside that constantly needed to please others, and staying peaceful even when chaos was inviting her into a tailspin. She had to learn to believe herself again—to believe that core of herself that knows she's valuable and worth caring for and that saying "no" can also be a way to express real love for yourself and others.

Marie's got some solid advice for those starting out: *Keep journaling. Keep writing, even when you don't feel like it.* The week she stopped journaling was the toughest one, so she got back at it again. Having that place to write offered time and space to get clarity, to process through difficult emotions, to find the truth she knew was in there. It wasn't an easy journey — but it was worth it. Here's some of what she's learned along the way.

Physical breakthrough: getting back on a workout and diet that nourishes her body, mind, and spirit. Part of returning home to ourselves after we've been away for a long time is that we realize all that we're hungry for — metaphorically and literally. We start to seek out the things that truly sustain us. We see and feel again how good it is to gently and intentionally tend the body that's been given to us to care for.

Emotional Breakthrough: drawing boundaries and

not getting mired in relationship drama. This was a huge leap forward, especially with her mom. Marie's relationship with her mom has been one of chaos, unpredictability, and upside-down care giving. Since she was a child, Marie watched her mother move from relationship to relationship. By the time Marie was an adult, her mother had been married eight times. She never really knew her biological father and was mostly raised by a stepfather. They moved constantly. Everywhere she went, she was always the new girl, always trying to make friends, always feeling insecure about who she was and where she belonged. Her mother was up and down so much emotionally that Marie did what a lot of kids do, she took on the role of an emotional stabilizer.

She made it her job to make sure her mom was okay — and when things weren't okay, Marie wondered, *Is this my fault? Did I cause this? Did I not do enough to keep her happy?* The cycle would continue. Before long, Marie didn't really have a sense of where other people ended and she began.

As you can imagine, it was a relationship that was extremely confusing for a kid — and for a grown-up, too. The boundaries around healthy interactions and caretaking were blurred at best, sometimes non-existent. Marie had very little confidence or ability to discern her own needs and often felt overwhelmed and powerless in the face of conflict with her mother. The default was always to make sure everything and everyone was okay — even if that meant she sacrificed her own emotional well-being.

Working through the book gave her new strength and a

new perspective. She started to draw lines that hadn't been clear before. There was one particular interaction that was very intense. "This drama — it could have been very long and dark in my mind," she said. "But I was able to handle the whole process in a more mature way. And I was able to move on." It was the moment she knew she was emerging from the suffocating shell that had been around that scared and confused little girl for so many years. She was learning how to *really* take care of herself.

Spiritual Breakthrough: making time for meaningful connection with herself and others, especially with her women friends. She took time to be with herself for the first time in ages. She said "yes" to friends, going out for a fun evening and for coffee, giving herself permission to sit, laugh, talk, and re-connect with people she cared about. Remember that Day 1 Story? Instead of telling herself that she should stay home, that it somehow wasn't okay for her to tend to those valuable relationships because other people needed her at all times (and needed her in ways that meant she couldn't care for herself) — she accepted the truth. The truth was that those who loved her were ready and willing to support and encourage her! Her husband said, "Go! Have fun!" So, she believed him — and she went. She had fun and got the chance to vitally reconnect with her friend.

And you know what else she (re)discovered? *When you tend to yourself, you get the energy you need to be able to tend to others in real, full, and generous ways.* When she was having coffee with another friend, a moment arose when she knew her friend needed support.

Because she had given herself time and space to tend

and nourish her own spirit in the past month, she found she had emotional and spiritual resources to be a supportive friend without feeling drained. "I was able to really be there for someone else — and I didn't see that one coming at all." Her smile is huge as she says this, shoulders back, head held high. Her voice is clear and strong. She's totally present to what taking care of herself means: It means being able to show up as the loving, giving, big-hearted person she was created to be. And she's glowing because of it.

Day 31 Story: *It's a good feeling to not overanalyze and second-guess every decision I make. Now, if I feel something, I can say it out loud. It's okay. I have a right to have a voice.*

Your Turn!

- Can you relate to Marie's challenges?
- What are some ways that *you* could reclaim your boundaries, your connection, your voice, and your genuinely generous heart in the next 31 days?
- If you did that, how could your story transform?

Signature yoga pose: *Pigeon.*

Why she loves it: *This is my favorite pose to practice for the simple reason that it feels so awesome on my hips!*

What I see when she is in this pose: I see a beautiful, strong woman who is surrendering into the moment and her greatness. She is bending in ways that aren't always the easiest, but she continues to choose herself and realizes the more she releases and sinks in deeper, the greater it feels.

Chapter 3

"Be patient toward all that is unsolved in your heart and try to love the questions themselves, like locked rooms and like books that are now written in a very foreign tongue. Do not now seek the answers, which cannot be given you, because you would not be able to live them. And the point is, to live everything. Live the questions now. Perhaps you will then gradually, without noticing it, live along some distant day into the answer."

— Rainer Maria Rilke

Gabby, Age 43

Superpowers: Her drive, determination, and strong will.

What was in her way: The need to control and have things be perfect — and how that was stealing her peace.

Day 1 Story: *I can't be happy unless I can plan for and control my future, and unless it turns out the way I think it should.*

It's almost impossible to see or talk to Gabby and imagine someone who was almost incapacitated by fear of the future. She is vibrant, younger looking than her 40 + years, brown hair pulled back in a youthful ponytail.

As she talks about the last year and the journey she's walked, you can see a seriousness in her eyes, in the way she holds her jaw sometimes. It's evident that taking an honest, intentional look at the last two decades has been a reckoning for her on many levels, and she's clearly still processing through that.

The difference now? *She's okay with the process*, and she doesn't have to know the outcome in order to feel confident that it will be alright.

Gabby's divine appointment with Essence of Life — and the path she's walked since being with the studio, with yoga, and with the book — started over a year ago. She started yoga classes as a way to be more present, more aware, and more accepting. To say she was struggling is an understatement.

The truth and her biggest challenge was that she often felt paralyzed by her perfectionism and self-criticism, her inability to let go, and her intense need for control. These were things robbing her of the chance to engage in the world fully and experience life. Her fear was robbing her of life. She was longing for some measure of peace — anything. So she started with yoga and eventually picked up a copy of the book. And with a lot of work, she's been uncovering peace, bit by bit, and life is shifting for her in some quiet but dramatic ways.

Physical breakthrough: re-inventing her relationship to food. If you've ever struggled with food, you know it is a physical issue because it's so immediate to your survival. It is not *only* a physical issue, it is highly complex and multi-dimensional. It's triggered by big and small interactions and is filled with self-judgment and self-punishment, which often perpetuates the cycle. It's incredibly difficult to break free from. Any sustained progress is a *huge* triumph.

Food was essentially the mask that Gabby used to resist facing what she was feeling, to fight any sense of being out of control. "My practice forever has been to take care of every emotion, good or bad, with food. You can see how that becomes a problem really quickly."

As someone who, for so many years sought the feeling of safety that comes with having control (even if it is an illusion that we have control over much at all!), Gabby always had a lot of rules around eating. There were "good" foods and "bad" foods, foods that were permitted and those that were strictly off limits. In those moments where she was triggered and ate a food that was on the "bad" list, she would immediately get angry and reprimand herself for doing wrong, a pattern of disordered eating that takes a huge toll on the mind and spirit.

Over the last 12 months as she has been facing demons and learning the long, tender art of real self-love, Gabby has experienced a new freedom with food. Though the practice of mindful eating has been very difficult, being present to that often-fraught intersection of food and emotion has been teaching her a great deal — and she's finding herself more and more open to the lessons. She's learning to let go of the tight grip she's had on emotional control, letting herself feel more authentic emotions when they arise — and letting herself take pleasure in eating without self-judgment or punishment. "I actually ate a cheat meal the other day. I ate the whole thing and didn't feel guilt or shame. I didn't feel the need to count calories or worry about what would happen, I just allowed myself to enjoy the moment. All of this I think comes from learning to love myself and feeling so much more comfortable in my own skin. I'd say that's a victory."

Emotional breakthrough: getting to gratitude as the default paradigm. Every family has its quirks and imperfections, and we all live in and contribute to our family's imperfections. When Gabby dove into the gratitude portion of *Pssst...Wanna Get Out of Your Own Way?*, she started to see how much judgment, criticism, and complaining had been a very normal part of her family dynamic, often leading to bitterness and resentment, even over small things. Going to the negative was the default.

"At first," she said, "I had to consciously push aside all the things that weren't going right to search for things I felt grateful for." But a strange thing happened; "As I did that more and more, the gratitude started to become a frame of mind." It points to the grace that becomes present in gratitude — that as we start to focus on what is going well, we also start to be more gentle with ourselves and others. It also shows that gratitude really is a *practice* — that is, we have to keep working at it for it to become natural to us.

Before Gabby started reading the book, she wasn't even consciously aware of where her mind went automatically. She wasn't present and was trying to grasp at control of every situation in her life. When things didn't turn out how she thought they should, she felt panicked, desperate, and angry. The diligent practice of gratitude has shown her the one thing — really, the *only* thing — she can control, and that is her perspective and her response to what happens. There's a palpable letting go in her voice when she says, "Now, I am able to recognize when I am coming from a place of negativity, and I can consciously turn it around."

Spiritual breakthrough: opening the door to forgiveness. Anyone who's faced a serious betrayal knows how difficult it can be to forgive. We often reflexively want to hold on — to our righteous anger, to control of outcomes, to our right to seek justice or revenge, to our right to feel wronged.

Gabby is totally honest when she says, "This is something that still challenges me. It's hard to forgive those who have hurt me."

Now here's the amazing breakthrough, in the process of working through the book, she realized two huge things: 1.) like most of us, she doesn't really understand what forgiveness actually is or how to do it, and 2.) deep inside, she really *wants* to learn how to forgive. She wants to surrender control, let go more, and open the door to living in a space that is softened by grace, gratitude, and forgiveness. That declaration of desire can change everything.

The other amazing breakthrough? She's willing to be gentle with herself in the midst of this very human, very messy, very imperfect process. She can't control all of it, and she knows there might be some bumps ahead — and she's still choosing to see herself as worthy of love and belonging in the middle of it all.

For so long, all Gabby has wanted is peace — and for so long, she thought the key to peace lay in having it all figured out. **Now, for the first time in her adult life, she's seeing clearly that the key to peace is in letting go of the need to have it all figured out, and being grateful for what *is* being revealed day after day.**

There's a slight catch in her voice — a moment of amazement, pride, and humble thankfulness. "I feel like I have come so far, and people in my life for many years, have noticed the change as well. I wouldn't have believed it was possible for me even four years ago. I'm very grateful that although I struggled with it for 40 years — I know I don't have to struggle for the next 40."

Day 31 Story: *You can't live a happy life **today** if you are too focused on the future. If you're open to learning from whatever comes your way, you'll always end up in a place that is right where you are supposed to be.*

Your Turn!

- Do you recognize Gabby's struggle for peace and surrender in your own life? If so, where and how?
- What are some areas in your life where you're making progress but that are still hard work for you?
- What are some ways you can frame the imperfect work as an opportunity to be gentle with yourself as you learn to love all that is unsolved and unknown in your life right now?

Signature yoga pose: *Tree.*

Why she loves it: *This pose has always made me feel centered and grounded, and for me, that makes this pose the essence of true balance. When I am positioned in this pose, I feel capable of creating balance in my own life.*

What I see when she is in this pose: I see a woman who is finding her roots to ground herself. She is allowing herself to reach higher towards her dreams. As she grows, she realizes how beautiful she is. Even though it is something we have seen in her all along, it is something she is learning to accept in her own mind. You can see her emerging confidence as she stands tall. Leaves change colors with the seasons — and like that, she is learning to flex and adapt her life when things don't go as planned, all while staying rooted in her own truth.

Chapter 4

There are three constants in life: change, choice, and principles.

— Stephen Covey, author of *The Seven Habits of Highly Effective People*

Charlie, Age 61

Superpowers: Knowing herself and what she wants, openness to new things, being a powerful source for action in her own life.

What was in her way: After two challenging years of being a full-time in-home caregiver, she felt herself succumbing to negativity, self-pity, and resentment.

Day 1 Story: *Life is pretty good, but some things are not working. How can I make it better?*

Charlie is not someone who struggles to know who she is, some of that might be her age. At 61, she's had a lot of life experience and time to figure out what makes her tick. She's a straight talker and you can hear a clarity in her voice that is deliberate and unapologetic. Picture the Swedish-American bombshell Ann-Margaret, with a ton of gorgeous red hair that's as fiery as she is, and that's Charlie. If she ever had a people-pleasing phase in her life, you can tell it's long gone now. She shows up, and if you approve of her — well, that's icing on the cake, but it's not going to determine how she presents herself or keep her from moving forward. It's nothing personal, but your opinion of her is none of her business, and she doesn't really have any interest in it. She is confident in herself and her life, and what you think can't change that.

Yoga and meditation, along with a wide variety of other fitness practices, have been central to Charlie's world for years. She is strong, agile, and powerful. That strength radiates out to all areas of her life. She's an avid traveler, an adventurer, an entrepreneur. She's used to calling the shots, and she likes it that way.

She made the choice early on in her life not to have children, even though it was an unusual choice for women of her generation. "I think it's very natural for a woman to not want to have kids. Some people say I'm selfish and self-absorbed for not having them, but that's not true at all." As an energetic, fun-loving woman who enjoys kids, she is naturally everybody's favorite auntie.

If you need any evidence that Charlie isn't selfish, you need only to look at the last few years. She cared for her father while he was dying, and she spent *two years* caring for her mother-in-law in her home after her mother-in-law's Alzheimer's made it impossible for her to live on her own.

This was the place where she met Jodie and started the

31-day journey with the book. In that first yoga class, she noticed something different about her teacher. Jodie freely walked around and wasn't afraid to make contact with the people in her class. "A lot of yoga instructors don't touch people because of liability fears, so you miss out on valuable opportunities to connect with people and to realign into the correct form. Jodie isn't like that. She has a really unique presence and energy in the room." Charlie knew she wanted to try the book.

Charlie's father had suffered deeply with his illness and although he remained joyful and positive throughout the dying process, losing him was a profound grief for her. In addition to that loss, she found her **biggest challenge** was that she was struggling with a lingering sense of negativity and resentment from having to navigate the intense care of her mother-in-law. "I needed to re-focus. I needed something to get me back." So she picked up a copy of the book and dove in.

Physical breakthrough: getting back to intentional self-care and re-imaging goals. As many Baby Boomers know, being a caregiver is an incredible exhausting occupation. As people are living longer, it's common for people to be sandwiched between caring for their children and caring for their parents. It can be draining on all levels, and sometimes taking care of yourself gets relegated to last priority. Charlie said simply, "I just needed to be reminded of the importance of self-love again. I knew it was there — I just needed to re-engage with the intentional practice."

She also had a moment when talking about fitness goals.

She decided that she wanted to be 122 pounds again. Jodie asked, "Why that number? Where did that come from?"

Charlie realized it was completely arbitrary and perhaps not all that reasonable. It was what she had weighed as a young woman, which really had no bearing on what her 61-year-old body wanted or needed. So instead, she reframed her goals around how she wanted to feel, what she wanted to wear, and things she wanted to do. This allowed her to fold the fullness of her *whole life* into the goal of being and staying healthy, not just some number from decades past. Instead of being punitive and self-criticizing, it was freeing and energizing.

Emotional breakthrough: opening the door to more abundance. Charlie has always enjoyed working and making money, and she's always looking for opportunities to break through to new levels. She likes to challenge herself and cultivate a sense of awareness around what's blocking her or getting in the way of new successes.

After going through Jodie's book, she tripled her income. **You read that right, *she tripled her income.*** How did she do it? "I decided to stop worrying about money and just look for opportunities to help others in a way that was coming from a wide-open, loving heart." This seemed to be key in attracting abundance of all kinds. When she kept her heart open, good things were able to flow in.

"Each day in the book, there's a different word to focus on," she said. "It was a simple exercise that just got me to notice the thoughts I was channeling." She knows that thoughts are powerful — they become our reality. "With that focus word, I could take a step back, process, and pay attention to self talk. When you open yourself to love, you allow good things to come into your life." It's a simple but profound moment to realize how much power we actually have to open or close opportunities for abundance of all kinds.

Spiritual breakthrough: reclaiming her life as a space for love, healing, joy, acceptance, and gratitude. While she was caring for her mother-in-law, Charlie started to notice something troubling; there was a negativity that was worming its way into their house, into her relationship with her husband, into the tiniest corners of her thoughts and life.

Charlie's mother-in-law has suffered a lifetime of depression that has gone untreated. She is what Charlie calls "a difficult personality" — someone who has always struggled to be happy and seemed stuck in cycles of anger and bitterness. Alzheimer's seemed to amplify these engrained characteristics, or perhaps it stripped away the filters — but her mother-in-law was routinely angry, manipulative, controlling, and combative. They were not close to begin with, and Charlie suddenly found herself in this role of being a 24/7 caregiver to someone whose emotional state was often quite toxic. It was taking its toll.

"I was absorbing all that negativity," she said. "I felt sorry for myself. I resented the fact that I was in this situation. I resented her and I resented my husband. I felt helpless, and I hated that feeling."

Going through the book made her realize that she had

options. She decided to take action. She knew she needed help and couldn't care for her mother-in-law at home anymore. She found and now pays for care at a memory-care center nearby. — It's a place with skilled and kind professionals who can gently care for Charlie's mother-in-law as her disease continues to progress and worsen. In addition to accepting that help, she's also been contacting state leaders to change legislation so that Alzheimer's care can be covered by Medicare. "It's so expensive, and Medicare pays nothing. Many families are in deep financial trouble, and it's something that needs to change."

Instead of feeling helpless, she's working on the small part that is hers to take care of. "Jodie's book got me to decide that I'm just going to take care of it and go, instead of throwing up my hands and saying I can't do anything." There was an obvious resolve and new energy in her voice. "This is not a problem that I'm helpless against — it's just an issue that needs to be taken care of. The moment I decided to stop feeling sorry for myself, things started turning around."

That action started a domino effect in her life. Things started improving at work, at home, and in her relationships.

Charlie and her husband, at first glance, might seem to be an odd pair. She's spiritually curious and believes in karma. Her husband, not so much. She loves meditation and yoga and Pilates. He plays hockey and has very little interest in the "woo-woo" side of things. She is flexible and open and likes to roll with it. He tends to want to control situations and events.

She pulls no punches when she says, "This is something

that requires daily maintenance on our part. We have to be intentional about loving each other despite — and sometimes because of — our differences."

When so much of her energy was going to dealing with the constant negativity she was encountering as a caregiver, she found she was less resilient and had a compromised ability to really *see, accept, and appreciate* her husband. As anyone who's done it knows, caring for a parent is difficult. But caring for an in-law has its own set of unique challenges. Charlie often saw things in a more black-and-white way — but she needed to practice acting with more intentional compassion and taking into account her spouse's perspective.

So although they had never stopped loving each other, the constant stress of caregiving had left them less connected. They were living in unison, but at a deep level they were distanced from one another. She knew that was something she wanted to transform. They loved each other and wanted to be partners and allies again.

Going through the book helped her to just stop and take a spiritual breath, and reconnecting with yoga and meditation reminded her of the power of acceptance. She had forgotten that there's always time to meditate. You can take two minutes to do deep breathing and that alone can do wonders in helping to slow down knee-jerk emotional responses. "I was able to let go again. I stopped trying to change him. He's just going about it in a different way. He's happy — it's not my job to tell him how to do things."

It's now been almost two years since her mother-in-law was moved to the memory care facility. In that time,

Charlie's father passed away. But even in the grief, she's found space again to make her life the way she wants it to be. "It's taken us a long time, but we've been able to get back. We found our way home again."

Day 31 Story: *You have to love yourself first. Live from love, joy, and gratitude — and amazing things will happen.*

Your Turn!

- Have you found yourself in a role that's eroding your ability to create or live your life fully?
- Are there areas where you could benefit from letting go of self-pity and resentment and boldly take action?
- How could reconnecting with self-love jump start that action?

Signature yoga pose: *Lotus.*

Why she likes this pose: *It centers her*

What I see when she is in this pose: I see a woman who is beautiful and Zen, yet who is still a wild child. She is the epitome of a woman with strength and power and has a goddess-like energy!

CHAPTER 5

This being human is a guest house.
Every morning a new arrival.

A joy, a depression, a meanness,
some momentary awareness comes
As an unexpected visitor.

Welcome and entertain them all!
Even if they're a crowd of sorrows,
who violently sweep your house
empty of its furniture,
still treat each guest honorably.
He may be clearing you out
for some new delight.

The dark thought, the shame, the malice,
meet them at the door laughing,
and invite them in.

Be grateful for whoever comes,
because each has been sent
as a guide from beyond.

—Rumi

Hope, Age 34

Superpower: Her insistent positivity and commitment to looking on the bright side.

What was in her way: Not knowing what to do with real, deep grief.

Day 1 Story: *This isn't how it's supposed to be — but I can power my way through.*

We hear a lot about the power of positive thinking — its ability to radically change outcomes, to put ourselves in the driver's seat when it comes to how our life turns out, to deliver to us the life we've dreamed of. We're told that anything's possible if we just believe in it enough.

Hope is someone who doesn't just *look* on the bright side. She *lives* there. She's incredibly upbeat, in tune, sparkling, and funny. She's active and loves to take care of herself. A natural optimist, she's had a can-do attitude her whole life, and it's served her well. Her upbringing was steeped in spiritual devotion and thinking. She was raised by committed Catholics and even has a number of great aunts who are nuns. She also has an innate spiritual curiosity within her, which has given her an appreciation for everything from her husband's Christian traditions to the notion of karma. She looks earnestly for meaning in all things and searches for God's purpose.

So what happens when something happens that has

no obvious explanation, that seems to make no sense whatsoever?

What happens when *nothing* you do — all the effort, positive thinking, and intentional action — changes the physical reality of what's going on for you?

What happens when that thing you can't make happen is the one thing you've wanted your whole adult life, almost more than anything else?

Suddenly, the bright side is painfully hard to find and feels out of reach.

That's been the reality Hope has been facing lately. **For seven years now, she's been standing face-to-face with the heartbreaking fact that things are not turning out the way she imagined and hoped they would. The grief of that — or, more specifically, the resistance to that grief — has been wearing her down and eating her up for a long time.**

Hope is married, with a 6-year-old "furry kiddo" named Brady the dog. She works as a high school counselor during the school year and at a golf course for fun during the summer. She loves her life, but she's recently been struggling with the fact that her life is missing the one big thing that she always expected, counted on and dreamed of.

"I always thought I would have two or three children," she says, looking down, her voice unusually quiet. "My husband and I started dating when we were 19, and it always seemed natural. We got married when we were 26, and while we were not trying to get pregnant at the time, we weren't using protection. But nothing happened."

What followed was six months of intentionally trying

to get pregnant — following advice from friends, and then a long string of doctor's appointments. The doctors found out that Hope had a small growth on her pituitary gland that was throwing her hormone levels out of whack and adversely affecting her fertility. Being super-positive Hope, she had no doubt that, since they knew what the problem was, they would be able to fix it. That's what doctors do, after all.

All told, she had three years of heavy medications to try and correct the hormone imbalance, and then two rounds of attempted in vitro fertilization (IVF).

She had no idea how exhausting and demoralizing fertility treatment can be. It started slowly, with medication for her hormone levels. The medication made her feel hung over every day, light headed, tired, nauseous, and uncharacteristically weak. She strictly followed the process for fertility treatments to boost egg production. She and her husband had sex exactly when the doctor told them to. There were more medications and shots.

"I was absolutely miserable. Every day I had a headache, felt nauseous and completely drained. The meds were changing my body, turning it into something it wasn't. I am an active person, but it hurt to be active. It was hard for me to accept bloating, and the pain, and not being able to do my workouts to their fullest. It was devastating. I felt like a sick person."

For a person who had always been unfailingly positive, putting so much relentless focus on something that *wasn't* happening, no matter how hard she tried to make that thing happen, was toxic for Hope. The drugs and the constant doctor visits made her inability to get pregnant the sole focus of her life.

At one point, her doctor recommended she get back to yoga to help her reconnect and get relief from the constant pain. It appealed to her spiritual side, as well as the part of her that really, *really* needed to do something physical, and it was gentle enough that her body could handle it.

That's how she found us at Essence of Life. At the end of class, when it was time for the Three Questions, she felt both nervous and relieved. For 18 months, she'd been essentially suffering alone. She had not opened up, to others or even to *herself,* about her experiences. In her tireless effort to stay positive, she hadn't really acknowledged how she felt deep down, or given expression to the intense grief that was running through her all the time as she saw her dream of motherhood slowly slipping away.

She realized this holding-in had taken an extreme toll. In addition to the very real physical symptoms generated by hormone-altering drugs, she felt herself sinking into despair. She was starting to become someone she didn't recognize. "I gave up everything to follow what the doctor needed me to do. It was all that was on my mind. I didn't have time to focus on anything else."

In class that day, answering the three questions — even though it was difficult and extremely vulnerable for her — she discovered a core truth about healing; when you find a safe place where you can acknowledge the big, scary thing you've been hiding from, just that single brave act of speaking it out loud can make it less big, and less scary.

She soon took home a copy of *Pssst...Wanna Get Out*

of Your Own Way? — and our journey together began. She was longing for peace of mind. She needed to face the fact that IVF was not working and get closure. She wanted to move forward, or at least to be able to ask what the next best step would be.

Physical Breakthrough: reclaiming her body. For someone who is naturally energetic, strong, and active, losing the ability to move freely can be devastating. It feels like you've lost the very essence of who you are when you can no longer energetically express yourself in that way. That's what it was like for Hope.

Add to that the debilitating physical side effects of the medications she was on, that compounded everything. She felt like she was living in a stranger's body. Yoga helped ease Hope back into her physical being again to some degree. Over time, she began to see that as long as she was still pursuing the IVF process, she was never really going to be "herself" again. She gave into the process & let "herself" try to be at peace.

And then, one day, she decided she'd had enough. After a particularly terrible morning, complete with running late, getting stopped by a cop, and dealing with a rude receptionist, she just felt...done. It all just felt like too much — too much sacrifice, too much negativity, too much unnecessary pain, too much disconnection from her true self and the life she longed for. She walked out and never went back. Yes, she was walking out of the office — but she was also walking away from the IVF process and staking a claim. She was going to get her life back. Somehow, she was going to find herself again.

Emotional breakthrough: reaching out, reaching in, and making a space for grief. In a strange way, Hope's positivity served as a kind of protective layer around her. As a naturally more private person, she could stay somewhat distant from uncomfortable relationships or situations and still be upbeat. She could "power through" challenges by herself with just sheer force of will — she rarely had to risk the vulnerability of reaching out and asking for support, or reaching in and honestly assessing how she was *really* feeling. It was almost as if the rosy outlook was a way of telling herself and others, *See? Everything's great. It's all good! Nothing to see here!*

We have a fundamental need to connect and express, and denying that has toxic effects on us over time, and Hope knew it. She felt the spark of connection in her first yoga class. The open sharing for the first time was as empowering as it was terrifying. She wanted more of that.

In Week 1 of *Pssst...*, Hope found the courage to reach out to her parents and express her appreciation for them. This was not an easy thing to do, she'd been distant from her mom for a while. They didn't always see eye-to-eye, and it was easier to just keep their distance than to reach out while working to maintain good boundaries. But the exercise was valuable — to just be there, to share her emotions, to take the time to tell them she cared. In fact, she resolved to contact the rest of her family and do the same. So that was one big step.

The biggest hurdle for Hope was just allowing herself

to grieve the unrealized hope of a house full of children, to mourn the idea of the life that she had lost. Because she prized being positive so much, the idea of grieving — of walking around just feeling *sad* — felt somehow wrong, like it would be self-indulgent. Plus, what was even scarier was the knowledge that the moment she let herself feel sad was the moment she would really, truly be letting go of the dream of having biological children.

As she worked through the book, she was finally able to let some of those feelings out. "I've realized it is okay to grieve. I didn't want to accept the fact that it was over, and that I was hopeful for things to turn around in my favor. I would try and keep myself from grieving, thinking that there was always hope for the future."

Throughout this grieving process, her emotions have run the gamut — angry, happy, sad, desperate, in denial, proud, resolute, hopeful. She has allowed herself to ride the tide of all of the stages. And she's learned what many in her situation have learned; that it is through giving ourselves permission to grieve that the pain starts to ease, that we begin to accept what is, to make peace with what has wounded us, to listen to what our grief is trying to teach us. It's how we begin, at last, after so much suffering, to see a way forward again.

Spiritual breakthrough: daily surrender, staying present, small steps. Hope is used to expecting big things. She sets outsized goals and moves towards them with focus and determination, she anticipates big shifts, big transformation. There's nothing wrong with ambitious goal setting, — but what Hope started to notice was that she was often *living* in some distant future where everything would turn out the way she had planned it. She often forgot that life — *her life* — was happening right here, right now.

When things didn't go the way they were supposed to with her fertility, her attachment to that future self created a huge amount of suffering. She associated "letting go" with giving up, with defeat, and she couldn't let herself do that. But in her dogged pursuit of that imagined future self, she wound up sacrificing important pieces of who she really was — her sanity, her happiness, her wholeness, her physical vitality, her sense of self-worth.

There is an intense bravery to what Hope has chosen in the process of working through the book. *She has chosen to embrace surrender.* She was afraid to open the book at the beginning, because she wasn't sure she was ready to change. "I wanted to believe everything was good, even though I knew it wasn't," she said.

She has put everything she believes and lives to the test, as she struggles to come to grips with the fact that she will not be able to have biological children. "It has changed my perspective of what I want to do with my life. A big part of me is missing every day with this decision. It feels like such a loss and it is so out of my hands. Honestly, it's just sad sometimes, even a year later. I have days where I see babies on Facebook and just cry. Then I have days where I see other women, older than I am, with no children, loving their lives. And I think about everything that's possible and I feel really grateful and excited."

The power is in seeing that *all* those ways of feeling are okay. It's okay to be sad, to be painfully uncertain about why this challenge has been given to her, to not understand why her dreams had to take on a different look. It's okay to welcome those moments where everything new seems possible, those moments where the new definition of her future self feels wildly exciting and full of life. It's all acceptable, all part of being human. Living a rich, full life isn't about having to be happy all the time. It's about embracing all of life in its ups and downs, its mess and beauty, and discovering who you want to be in the midst of it.

In this way, Hope has discovered that the power of positive thinking is less about denying difficult feelings and more about trusting that you will survive and be transformed by pain, that you will be stronger and more whole as a result of the challenges you've faced.

To her surprise, even going through the book was a reminder of the power of small steps. Instead of some seismic shift, she feels like she's simply discovered a better version of herself in taking in that gradual healing process as it showed up each day.

This version of herself is more free, more courageous. She focuses more on the little things, and the joy in the moment, instead of constantly focusing on some far-off goal. "I feel like there's been a switch in my focus — looking at being present in the moment and taking in all of the amazing things I already have in life in front of me, instead of fixating on this idea of what I 'should' have in life."

That includes focusing on the opportunities she has all around her to share her amazing, beautiful heart with kids and other people who really need her. She's giving her all to the high school kids she counsels. She's engaging more as an aunt and godmother. She's opening her heart — including the difficult moments — to give extra love to her friends' children. She's offering her story openly as a way to connect with, receive encouragement from, and empathetically comfort others who are walking this path. She's using her own walk in the shadows as a way to bring light to others.

At the end of her journey with the book, her goal is as simple and as bold as this; *My goal is to say yes.*

Yes to life. Yes to *all* of it, whatever that looks like, one day at a time.

It's a goal that is firmly rooted in the Now. It's how small things add up to huge transformation.

Day 31 Story: *As I move through my journey, I have learned acceptance of where I currently am, and not where my planned destination may be. There is joy and pain in that acceptance. But this is just a part of my journey, a step. Disappointment can be painful — but it does not define me.*

Your Turn!

- Have you struggled to let in *all* of life? Are there some feelings or experiences you're afraid to experience fully?
- What could happen if you allowed those difficult emotions to be gentle teachers to you in your journey?

Signature yoga pose: *Wild Child into Backbend.*

Why she loves it: *This pose makes me feel fully connected, yet challenged and out of control at the same time. There is this moment that happens when I'm in wild child that I'm stuck wondering if I am strong enough to catch myself while falling. But then I decide to take a chance and throw my body into it. In that split second, my fear turns to accomplishment as my fingers find the floor as my pelvis and chest lift upwards towards the sky. There I am, in my backbend, soaking up the glory of achievement, and in that moment all seems to be at peace again.*

What I see when she is in this pose: I see a beautiful woman who had to gain courage to step beyond points in her life that she never thought she would have to. There is this sense of a wild child that resides within her, yet her spirit is so nurturing. I love to watch her move in yoga. Just like in life, she has learned to transition beautifully though the motions!

CHAPTER 6

Coming together is a beginning; keeping together is progress; working together is success.

— Henry Ford

Claire, 37, and Frank, 43

Superpower: Committed to healthy living, outrageous positivity, sparky and dedicated love.

What was in their way: For Frank — coming to terms with mortality and finding the courage to follow his bliss. For Claire — overcoming anxiety and fear from the past.

Day 1 Story: *Things are great — we have a lot going for us. What could take our relationship and life from good to extraordinary, empowered, and joy-filled?*

It's not hard for Frank and Claire to be the center focus of a room. They are both powerhouses — physically and socially — and together they have a palpable energy that follows them like a light. They love life, and they love each other to pieces. They're a team, wherever they go and whatever they do.

Frank is a typical New Yorker. Stocky, but solid and lean, and someone who lives life out loud. He's a weightlifter and it's clear he takes care of himself. He exudes an affable quality - a steady confidence. Underneath everything, he is what Claire calls "a big ol' teddy bear" — someone who cares deeply, shows affection, someone you feel safe around.

Like Frank, Claire values good health and gives time to eating well and exercising. A petite blond bombshell, she has a megawatt smile like a flint. It ignites warmth and enthusiasm everywhere she goes. It was the thing that drew Frank to her in the first place, the thing he couldn't forget after their first meeting. "I love her smile," he says with a goofy grin. "It just draws you in." When you're in her presence, she has the unique ability to put her focus entirely on you so that you feel truly seen and heard.

When they're together and you're with them, you feel like you've been invited to the party, like you're family, like you belong.

You might imagine these two as perfect personal trainers, or high-powered business people. But their deep hearts and passion for service brought them both into the world of education. Claire is a school counselor with a psych background whose main goal is to connect meaningfully with her students. Given her past experiences, she is highly empathetic. She often knows exactly what kids are going through and seeks to provide them with a safe space to share, be themselves, and get the help they need.

Frank has spent his professional career as a special

education teacher and coordinator at a charter school that serves inner city kids. Many of the kids he works with are in survival mode — generational poverty, violence and addiction in the home, no safe foundation, often not enough food or reliable shelter. He willingly pours himself into watching over them, loving them, showing them their value. Beyond school hours, he is setting up an after-school program with his kids to go through *Psst...Wanna Get Out of Your Own Way?* — as a way for them to grow, but also just to give them a safe place to get a meal and have a roof over their heads for a couple more hours a day.

Frank and Claire share an incredible, true love. Theirs is a story of redemption and second chances. They've both experienced pain and setback, and death has visited them both, in different but profoundly transformative ways. Part of what makes their story so powerful is their unwavering commitment to each other through the healing process, how they have held each other up, and how clearly they are devoted to the growth and fulfillment of the other.

Claire was the classic firstborn. The oldest of four kids, she describes her childhood as loving and safe. She enjoyed high school, was social and popular, and met her first husband there at 19. By the age of 23, Claire was married and already a school counselor. She'd finished her Psych degree and immediately jumped into doing work she loved. She was dedicated and disciplined.

When Claire was 29, home for Christmas break, her parents told her that a large sum of money had been withdrawn on a debit card they hadn't used in ages. They were naturally confused and concerned that the card had been stolen. It had been stolen, but not by a random criminal. They soon discovered that Claire's younger sister — a college student on the dean's list — had become addicted to the painkiller oxycontin (she tried it after her boyfriend had been prescribed the medication after a car accident), and later to heroin, and was stealing money to fund her habit.

The family rallied, and after a few tries, her sister successfully completed treatment. It was Spring, and things seemed to level out.

Then, Claire's sister suddenly dropped off the radar and stopped speaking to her family. In October, Claire got a call that she needed to go to her parents' house. She was panicked and worried, knew it had to do with drugs, but the news she received was not what she ever thought she'd hear.

Her sister, then only 24, had returned to heroin and had been selling herself as an escort in order to buy drugs. The full truth is that her boyfriend, the one who had introduced her to oxycontin, was actually pimping her out to get money for their drugs. Shortly after she began prostituting, a convict who had been out of prison less than a year hired her as an escort, and the night went horribly wrong. He tied her up and murdered her in the second story room of a housing complex. While she was fighting for her life, her boyfriend was in the parking lot, waiting for her to return with money so they could get more drugs.

The neighbors in the building heard screaming and had called the police. In an attempt to escape, the murderer jumped out the second story window and fled. He was later caught, convicted for the murder, and is currently back in prison.

Claire was already a person who highly valued safety, control, and predictability. The grief of losing her sister, especially under such horrific circumstances, increased her anxiety and fear dramatically. She always worried that each phone call was going to bear more bad news about her loved ones. She fought to keep normal stresses from escalating into panic.

Her husband at that time, while a decent person, also shared these high-anxiety traits. At work, he was plugged in, but at home, he was disconnected. They found that they fed each other's negative energy. Claire spent so much of herself trying to be his cheerleader that she lost herself in the process and forgot her own self-care. After several more years, they finally separated.

Claire, who had naturally been a positive person growing up, felt stuck. On the surface she was bubbly, socially active and engaged in her world. She loved working with kids and was great at her job. She had a huge, compassionate heart for service. Anyone who met her would think she really had it all together. But underneath, she still struggled with anxiety. She longed for more balance and peace in her life but wasn't sure how to get there.

She had been divorced for five years when she first met Frank at a beer and wine festival. Frank was recently divorced and was raising his ex's kids, along with his own 14-year-old daughter from his first marriage. Claire and Frank clicked and had a good conversation, but nothing happened until the next year. They met again at the festival, and this time, they went out on a date. And another. And another. They quickly knew that they were meant to be in each other's lives.

"She's mushy and all lovey-dovey," says Frank, laughing. "And, as it turns out, so am I."

Claire was immediately drawn to his steadiness, his ability to roll with life. She felt a stability with him that had not been present before and appreciated how he challenged her to look at her own coping mechanisms in the face of the unknown.

They had been together for six months when, at only 42 years old, Frank had a massive heart attack and nearly died. What started at 5am as an achy shoulder landed him in the hospital where doctors told him that he was in the middle of a life-threatening heart attack. "It felt like there was a massive hand on my chest, burrowing its fingers into my bones." Surgeons performed an emergency angiogram and put a stent in one artery that was 100% blocked. Another was blocked 80%, and another 30%. Doctors told him they thought with meds, those blockages could be improved.

He knew his body held the genetic potential for something like this. His father had had a few heart attacks, six bypasses, two valve replacements, a stroke, congestive heart failure, and was blind in one eye. Frank was strong, healthy, active, and ate well. He didn't quite believe it could happen to him.

The entire time, Claire was by his side. "It scared the living hell out of me. I thought for sure he was going to die." They had only been together half a year, but they knew that this event had shown them clearly what was most important in life.

Frank said, "We knew in that hospital room we were ready to get married."

Several months after the heart attack, Frank and Claire met up with me and decided to go through *Pssst...Want to Get Out of Your Own Way?* together. With all the stresses of planning a wedding and blending two lives together, they knew they wanted to stay focused on being a team. And as counselors, they understood the importance of taking time to work on issues together — so they decided to go through the book as a form of pre-marital counseling. It was exciting to have a couple committed to taking the journey at the same time, and they seemed ready to go. They looked at the first three pages, and they knew they were all in. "I read those pages," said Frank, "and I thought, *This is what's going to keep me alive.*"

Their **main challenges** were both around healing, but of different kinds.

Claire wanted freedom from her fear and anxiety. She wanted to worry less about always keeping people happy, wanted to stop being afraid of upsetting anyone. She wanted the confidence to be calm and to show up as herself, no matter what.

After his heart attack and not being in his normal fitness routine, Frank wanted a lifestyle shift. "I want to move to a more plant-based diet, get back to lifting, clear my mind." With a stressful job and the looming specter of genetic heart problems, he knew it was essential for him to learn how to effectively decompress and focus on the positives. In addition, after the heart attack, doctors put him on a raft of medications — two blood thinners, cholesterol meds, pills for high blood pressure, even though he doesn't have high blood pressure. He set an ambitious goal of getting off all meds except baby aspirin.

Both of them had the immediate sense that their finding each other and this book was choreographed by the Universe. "We're ready to dive in, to meet change, and to grow even closer."

Physical breakthrough: re-evaluating nutrition and exercise for a heart-healthy lifestyle. Even though Frank can't do 100% of what he was doing before, he can do 85% — which is pretty amazing less than a year after suffering a massive heart attack. He's been cleared to get back into weightlifting.

Getting into yoga has been a huge benefit for both of them. They now schedule "yoga date nights," and they've both seen improvements — more relaxed, more connected, more flexible, better sleep. "I was more into hard exercising before, and I kind of resisted yoga as a sort of soft workout," Frank admits. "But it's hard work, and good work. It's helped me focus and has really given me a way to deal with stress in my life."

They've also shifted their eating to more plant-based proteins, which has contributed to improved arterial bloodflow and a reduced need for medications.

In their busy schedules, sometimes they helped each other reach daily goals. "It was like a game," Claire smiles.

"It was spontaneous and fun, helpful, energetic, and just so positive." Working together helped them to see what a great team they are and how they can be an encouragement to one another through anything.

Emotional breakthrough: reduced anxiety, learning to ask for help, letting their guard down. "The cool thing about this book," said Frank, "is that it's really just about re-focusing on simple things. You do little things every day, and by the end of a month, you've made huge gains."

Claire echoes that feeling. "It's a great reminder to be grateful every day. It's so helpful to have that daily reminder to create *habit* of making goals, a *habit* of gratitude, a *habit* of noticing what's working."

The journaling was a big help for both of them in the process — having that motivation and that regular reminder of what they wanted to put their energy towards. It kept the focus manageable, one day at a time in a frenetic world.

For Frank, the breakthrough came when he realized that he had never in his life had to rely on anyone. He was a self-made man. He didn't ask for help. He just muscled through. "But, you know, a heart attack brings you to your knees, literally and figuratively. I had to reassess everything. God weaves this huge tapestry, and brings the right people in at the right time to help and teach — but we have to be willing to see and receive it." In the 31 days, he saw clearly that Claire was here to help him, and it was his job to open up to that, to let his guard down instead of just trudging on alone.

Claire found a new freedom from constant worry.

Her anxiety levels dropped, which was huge for her. She developed and practiced skills that helped her temper her fretfulness by allowing herself to just rest fully in each moment. At one point, she even coached herself into telling someone she couldn't make a social commitment. For many people, this is not a big deal. But for someone who struggles with anxiety and who puts massive amounts of energy into not upsetting others — to simply say "no" without freaking out is a *major* accomplishment. "I realized, it's okay to just say *I can't*. Saying no is just as important as saying yes. You have to fill yourself up in the same way you fill others. Nurturing your own soul is just as important as nurturing another person."

They found that in working together, their own connection deepened. They sat together at breakfast and reflected and went over goals. They held each other accountable and cheered each other on. "We knew we were doing well," said Frank, "but we also saw that there's room for improvement, room to grow — and that's great. We have so much more to learn, and it's cool to know we can look forward to getting closer and closer as we work together."

Spiritual breakthrough: taking risks, seeking purpose, inviting change in each day. Frank acknowledges that he was spiritual before. He grew up Methodist and practiced different avenues of faith throughout his life. He has always felt that there's a bigger force out there keeping an eye on us. But his heart attack definitely opened him up in a visceral way to a universal truth, all we ever have is today, right now. "Who knows when our time's up? You have to live life 100%, with no regrets."

Part of living fully has been to look intentionally at what he loves and wants to do. He had to go back over the last decade to see how he got to where he is. While he likes his work, he also got thrown into taking on an additional administrative role — which he did not seek out or apply for — that has come with tons of extra time, energy, anxiety, and internal politics that drag him down. He recognized that the constant strain and pressure of basically working two full time jobs in a high-stress environment — both as a teacher and as an administrative special ed coordinator for the school — had been negatively affecting his health over the last several years. While going through the book, he asked himself point-blank - *What do I want my day to day life to be built on? What's my foundation?* He had to go back and assess what he truly wanted for himself and his life with Claire.

What he realized was this: he wants more fun, more curiosity, more flexibility, the chance to be his own boss.

He's always had a passion for brewing beer, and in the back of his mind, he's always thought about opening his own facility. But he kept dismissing it as nothing serious. Now? He's got clarity: "Before it was just a dream, but now it's like, *Screw it. Let's make this happen.*" Sometimes "screw it" is the most daring spiritual revelation you can have!

Claire is supportive and excited for whatever is ahead. As she spent 31 days focused on one day at a time, she started to see the benefits of rooting herself in the present, not fretting about what is ahead, but welcoming each opportunity for transformation as it knocks. "You have to do the work — this is not a quick fix. It's a daily journey, because your life changes daily."

When you sit with Claire and Frank, you get this sense of a sort of Divine appointment. It's not hard to believe that these two were meant to find each other at the time they did, that they are each other's teacher, and that the immense challenges they've faced individually have served the purpose of uniting them in the most powerful way possible.

Their journey didn't stop at the end of the book, of course. Claire reported that they both liked some of the exercises so much that they've kept doing them, months later.

Frank sums it up from this journal entry: "I'm grateful for my soul mate. Being with her makes me stronger." They grew individually, and as a couple. "We fell in love even more, and I can't wait for what's ahead."

Day 31 Story: *Let's make this real. Not "someday," but* **this** *day.*

Your Turn!

- Has your life been shaped by some massive, unexpected event? What do you think that event might be trying to teach you?
- What role can your loved ones — whether that's a partner, a close friend, or a family member — play in helping you heal, grow, and reclaim your freedom?

Claire's signature yoga pose:. *Tree.*

Why she loves it: *When I am in this pose, it reminds me to keep balance in all aspects of my life.*

What I see when she is in this pose: I see an incredibly rooted, alluring woman with these captivating branches that wrap love, beauty, and growth around everyone she knows.

Frank's signature yoga pose: *Lunge.*

Why he loves it: *This pose makes me feel strong and mighty. When I am in this pose, it also inspires me to want to take care of myself for a healthy and strong future.*

What I see when he is in this pose: I see a strong, powerful man who is willing to get down onto his knees to help anyone he can. He holds within him the power of a giant, a power so strong it can lift any soul.

CHAPTER 7

Throughout all of history, people have been
fascinated with feats of superhuman strength.
We're told tales of gods that move mountains
and men that wrestle lions with their bare hands.
But in truth, the most heroic acts of all are the
weights everyday people lift within themselves.

—Beau Taplin, author and musician

Josephine, Age 26

Superpowers: Amazing resilience, strong will, love for God, big dreams.

What was in her way: Her struggle to accept her past as she was facing the reality of starting over.

Day 1 Story: *I am not worth taking care of. Nobody sees, understands, or supports me. I'm alone, and I'm a failure.*

Joey's story is really about the power of perspective. There's no question that she's made some radical changes in her life and environment — you'll see that clearly as you read on — but so much of the huge shift for her in the course of doing the book has come in *how* she sees what is and what has been. There's an incredible strength you can claim when you realize that when you change your perspective, you really can change everything — even yourself.

At 25, Josephine (or Joey for short) was living a life that wasn't anything like the life she had imagined for herself growing up. She had a baby while she was still really young. Instead of the career she hoped for, she had a job working nights managing a fast food restaurant.

But the most difficult thing was her marriage. Her husband — the father of her child — was often verbally, and sometimes physically, abusive. Like many women in her situation, she told herself over and over again that her happiness was not that important. On the worst days, she repeated in her head: *My son deserves his parents together, and this is going to be my life. It doesn't matter that I'm not happy.*

She told herself that when she felt alone. She told herself that when she got run over at work, breaking three bones in her foot — and after finishing her night shift, her husband refused to take her to the hospital, pick her up, or help her at home when she couldn't stand or walk. She told herself that when he was berating her, ignoring her, pushing her around.

She finally realized she needed to get out when she saw that she was no longer the only one affected by the abuse. Her son, who was three at the time, started cowering, looking down, hiding behind her or under the table when her husband would go on rampages.

She just wanted to escape. But like many women in that situation, she didn't know how. Where would she go? What about her son? She feared her family would never support her decision to leave her husband.

Joey started making plans to move out. But it was much more complicated than she first anticipated. Everything they owned, she had paid for. All of it — the house, the car, everything. But it was all in her husband's name. And since she couldn't work because of her injuries from the accident, she didn't have any money to make a new start. Legally, she had nothing.

She wanted to buy some time to make more money, but her husband's anger was escalating, and she knew she couldn't safely remain there any longer. For an instant, she thought about moving back in with her mom. But a stubborn voice inside panicked; *No way. You **cannot** move back in with Mom. Not at 25 with a son in tow.*

She paused, but just for a moment. Over the years, she had put so many blocks in place in her relationship with her mother, that it was nearly impossible for her to assess objectively what was going on. She looked at her son, and she knew. If she wanted to keep him safe, she'd have to create a small door within the walls she'd constructed regarding her mom and go to the only safe place she knew, regardless of her personal resistance.

So, with nowhere else to go, she finally made the move to her mother's. She had no idea then that this decision would be the first step towards her lifelong freedom.

In one way, there was great relief to finally being in safety. But instead of starting to feel better, that's when Joey finally hit bottom. "I felt horrible after moving back in with my mom. It's definitely not where I wanted to be at 25 years old, living back with my mother. I was just really depressed. It was a good two weeks where I was in my room, alone, sobbing."

As is common in post-trauma situations, Joey felt completely unanchored. Yes, she was free — but she was away from anything familiar. She had no routine, no one to come home to, nothing to depend on. Even if it was bad before, it was a misery she *knew.* This was a misery she was wholly unfamiliar with.

Like many abuse victims who feel they are alone in their situations, Joey felt like there was no one to help her deal with the pain she was feeling, so she worked hard to hide the painful reality of what she was experiencing. Out in the world, she put on a happy front, but inside she was desperate and hurting. She never went to therapy or any kind of counseling. She didn't have any practice reaching out for help, and had been conditioned to believe over the years that no one cared, no one would show up, and that she was totally alone. Even her deep faith in God brought her no comfort. She prayed every day, but felt like she didn't have that connection to God anymore. She felt empty, like she was just saying the words, but no one could hear her. It was alienating, isolating, painful, and extremely lonely.

Joey *thought* that her biggest challenge was getting away from her husband, but she soon realized, with a sinking feeling that **her biggest challenge was facing the pain of abuse and the terror of starting over again on her own. Her biggest obstacle to happiness now was herself.**

It was about this time that she happened to show up at my book signing party. Joey had for many years been a part of my life, and I have known her since she was young. The Universe has a funny way of allowing people to flow in and out of our lives at the right moments. Joey saw a Facebook post about the book signing and felt an urge to be there that she didn't fully understand. For the first time in ages, she got up, did her hair, put on clean clothes and some makeup, and showed up to the signing.

She picked up the book and saw the words on the cover, *Pssst...Wanna Get Out of your Own Way?*

Something landed. She thought, *Yeah, I really do.*

So she took a copy home.

She was desperately looking for a way to re-make her life. She was not at all where she wanted or hoped to be. "I went through a lot, and when I chose to be with this man, I didn't think I would be living with my mother at the age of 25. I wanted a career — I didn't want to be working at a fast food restaurant. I wanted to be done with school, wanted to know where I was headed, wanted to be in a career that I was going to have until retirement, or at least be on the road to getting there."

She felt like a complete failure, and totally lost. She had so much guilt, anger, and depression. She knew deep down that the first — and most difficult step — was not going to be about becoming a different person, but *learning to genuinely love who she was right now.*

At that moment, it felt impossible. But that's the good thing about starting at the bottom. You have nowhere to go but up.

Physical breakthrough: tending to herself and her body again. Almost from the moment she opened the book, it started pushing Joey in directions she never really thought about going before.

It's very common for abuse victims to practice a kind of disassociation from themselves and their bodies. They're in survival mode, and often their focus is on protecting their children. They literally forget about themselves. "I was always caring about everyone else. I've never been the kind of person to look at myself and appreciate what I am. I started noticing that every single page of the book was, 'What are you thankful for?' That's just something that I wasn't used to." When she first saw the gratitude question, she just stared at it for a good 20 minutes. She didn't know what to say.

Goals were easy — or so she first thought. She knew where she was, and she knew she didn't want to be there.

And when she had to write down what she liked about herself? "I couldn't look at myself and see good things. I was so angry with myself. It was just a really, really bad place."

As hard and painful as it sometimes was, Joey stuck with the book — and started to experience some surprising results. For one, she started doing yoga because of the book. She had yoga tapes but had never touched them. Once she was reading the book, she decided to give them a try — and discovered that yoga helped her feel better and stronger.

After the accident, Joey had been unable to exercise, because she couldn't put any pressure on her foot. She gained a lot of weight, which wasn't doing much to help her struggling self-esteem. But now, she had finally found a way to take care of her body that worked for her. She had a way to take time to just focus on her physical being, to be with her body in loving ways, to tend to and honor all the places that were hurting.

And it wasn't just her body that was starting to feel better.

Emotional breakthrough: falling in love with herself — for the first time — and experiencing all the ripple effects of that in her life. A strange thing happens when we slow down just long enough to be kind to ourselves again; we start to notice and appreciate the kindness. We start to realize how good it feels to be tender, to give ourselves grace, to make peace.

Joey started to see a difference. "I've seen a pattern in my journaling where I have been choosing to say something good about myself daily, rather than looking at the negative or waiting for someone or something else to make me feel good."

And it began to move out from there, because when you shift how you see *yourself*, other people also start to appear differently, as well. Things started to fall into place with her mother, someone she admired but didn't feel necessarily close to. She's always been a daddy's girl and thought that her mom didn't always understand her. But she started to realize that it wasn't that she didn't understand — it was that Joey was holding back because she was a version of herself that she didn't really want her mother to know.

All that is evolving into something new. "I feel like now we can just sit down together and talk. It's been years since we have been able to do that. I'm experiencing her as more supportive — but in hindsight, maybe she always was, and in my mind I was feeling judged and not supported, because I judged myself so harshly all the time. It's crazy how when you change your perspective, relationships change."

Loving herself has allowed her to show up as a steadier, stronger parent. She used to let her son get away with everything, because she saw how limited he was around his dad. But now she sees the value in setting good boundaries for him and how that has strengthened their trust and bond.

It's amazing to see the outward expansion of true self-love. The body responds to intentional care. So does the heart. So does the spirit.

Spiritual breakthrough: forgiving, letting go, and finding God again by finding the teacher in a difficult past. This was a huge moment, the day Joey felt reconnected to God and to her spirituality. She felt a deep emptiness, an abandonment. She prayed, but it felt like it just went into nothing. As someone who had placed such a value on her spiritual life, this emptiness was devastating and lonely.

But strangely, God showed up in the midst of her gratitude. In the midst of her learning to love herself. In the midst of her facing and accepting her past. She saw a similar pattern emerging when she moved and adjusted her lens. Suddenly, so many things that had seemed absent started to come into focus.

On Day 14, she said it out loud, "What I like about myself is my faith, that through my darkest days I can see God's light." The Light was there all along — it was her transformed perspective that gave her new eyes to see.

After walking through so much darkness, these days Joey seems to radiate a new brightness. She holds herself higher. She smiles and looks people in the eye. She speaks her mind. She's found love again in a new relationship — only this time, she brought a deep, real love for herself to the process, which has transformed what dating looks like.

Part of what's kept her on track is that she's continued right on with the journaling, even though she finished the book. That has helped keep her focus on gratitude and making peace with difficulties. "Every day I could work on myself a little bit more without trying to force myself. Going through this book daily, I found the ability to let go of the anger I had around what I'd been through. I've learned not to hate what I've been through, but instead find what there is to learn and use it as strength for where I'm at today."

Day 31 Story: *I can stand up for myself and be strong. I don't live in fear of transition in life. My mindset has changed from* **Oh no, what am I going to do?** *to* **I am going to do this. Bring it on!** *I know I am strong. I am confident. I am loved.*

Your turn!

- Are you finding yourself at a place where you have to start over?
- Do you feel stuck in anger or resentment of the past?
- What might shift for you if you were able to let go of that anger and receive something else?

Signature yoga pose: *Cobra*

Why she loves it: *It really gives my back an amazing stretch in the morning before I start my day.*

What I see when she is in this pose: I see a child that I've known since birth, blossom into a beautiful woman. Rising up with her head held high and an open heart, I watch her learning how to strengthen herself spiritually, physically, and emotionally as she faces this life journey!

CHAPTER 8

*Although you should not erase your responsibility
for the past, when you make the past your
jailer, you destroy your future. It is such a great
moment of liberation when you learn to forgive
yourself, let the burden go, and walk out into a
new path of promise and possibility.*

— John O'Donohue, poet

Aurora, Age 59

Superpowers: Resilient, hard-working, independent woman and single mother.

What was in her way: Shame from the past and a deep-down sense of unworthiness that has caused her to say no to real happiness.

Day 1 Story: *If you don't make the "right" choices in the moment, you don't really deserve happiness.*

Aurora is what her name suggests, a beam of light. Her smile radiates. She is quick to laugh and her eyes spark with intelligence and strength. Her bobbed gray hair frames a face that is both gentle and resolute. She has a look that says *I can do anything.* And she has done an amazing amount — mostly on her own.

Aurora has lived an extraordinary life. She was one of nine siblings growing up poor in her hometown. Her biological father was an abusive alcoholic. Her mother remarried when Aurora was five. As a girl raised in a very traditional Catholic Mexican family, there were certain social, religious, and cultural expectations for her — that she would be a good girl, that she would grow up, make her family proud, get married, have babies.

Instead, longing for adventure and something different, she left home, went to three years of college in a nearby city, returned home, joined the military, and enjoyed a 26-year military career traveling the world and sowing wild oats. During that time, she got pregnant and raised a daughter, now 32, on her own, in the military, on a single salary. Needless to say, that was not a common, or much understood choice, for women in the 1970s. Her family didn't always support her. People in her town talked.

You can see pride in Aurora's face as she talks about her strength, her ability to overcome and rise above, the joy she takes in her strong, independent daughter. But there is a loneliness, too. There were times when she was close to love, to marriage, to companionship — but she always backed out at the last minute. "There was a part of me that always thought it must be false, that no one could really love me like that," she said. "I always believed that happily ever after was not for me — it was for other people, but not for me. I guess I didn't think I was attractive enough, didn't think I deserved it." So, when the time came to say yes to love, she backed out, thinking they'd just leave, anyway. She figured she'd just save them the trouble. Aurora laughs self-consciously as she says this, but it rings with a kind of hard truth. When we don't believe we deserve something, we'll sabotage our own happiness again and again.

That's where Aurora was when she found us at Essence of Life. "I want to forgive myself for the times I messed up. And I want to stop feeling shame for the things that happened to me that I had no control over, for the things I didn't know when I was younger." It's the first time her eyes lose their spark, as she looks down and contemplates her mug of tea. It's been a heavy weight to carry all these years.

This encapsulates Aurora's **main challenge:** giving herself the gentle space to forgive, to let go, to see herself as truly worthy of love and happiness. She took on the *Pssst... Want to get Out of Your Own Way?* challenge somewhat out of curiosity — but also out of a deep longing to find her way back to herself again.

"At first, I thought, *Oh, man. Does this mean I'm gonna have to be all brutally honest and stuff?*" Aurora laughs and shakes her head as she says this — but she headed into the book like she has with so many life challenges: head on, with courage. "I realized even if I had to be brutally honest, it would probably be good for me. So I just jumped in."

Physical breakthrough: tending to self-care and the things that make her feel good. Aurora has proven many times that she's strong on the inside. She wanted a yoga and Pilates routine that would strengthen her outside, as well. Even though it's clear what a beautiful person she is, she's always felt she wasn't worthy of being seen as attractive. This has often led her to make choices around eating and exercise that don't serve her. The wonderful thing about yoga is that it is a physical practice that asks us to be fully present in our bodies. Through that regular appointment, just showing up and paying attention and learning to appreciate what we are and what our bodies can do — a whole new relationship with the body develops. And Aurora has felt that, too. You don't exercise so that you'll feel worthy and "good enough." You move your body *because* you're worthy. Intentional movement is a way that we thank our bodies for being everything that they are.

Emotional breakthrough: learning that it's okay to put herself first. Parents know this, and single parents have a special window into this reality. It's so easy to forget that your needs matter, too. Even after kids are grown and living independently, it's difficult to realize that they are just that, grown and independent. Even though Aurora's daughter is in her 30s now and quite successful, Aurora found herself continuing to put off major life choices around work and money, because she was worried about having enough to support her daughter.

Through her work with the book, she finally realized that she'd done her job, and she'd done it well. She'd raised a responsible, capable daughter who is fully able to support herself. "I've always thought of her as young. But she's not. She's a woman. She's got enough smarts and resources to take care of herself."

This epiphany has opened up another joy for Aurora, she has choices again. If she wants to work, she can. If she doesn't, she doesn't have to. She can focus on saving and traveling again and trying new things. She can take adventures and trust that the good work she did with her daughter will be enough. For someone who has spent three decades in the trenches of single motherhood — where she was the sole provider on one salary and absolutely everything depended on her — this is a huge revelation that opens up worlds of possibilities.

Spiritual breakthrough: that terrifying, liberating journey of forgiveness. In those early years in the military, Aurora explained her choices like this, "I went completely crazy." Having lived under such restriction and crushing expectation at home to be a good Catholic girl, the freedom that she felt when she left home was exhilarating. She also had no idea how to handle it. She was lonely and afraid and longing to belong and feel loved.

In the military, and in her work as a secretary, Aurora was often the one woman in a boys' club culture. Like so many other women, she experienced unwanted advances, degrading treatment, and worse. And she knew what women knew then: you don't talk about it. You don't complain. You don't make a fuss. The one time she complained, there was retribution at work, and she feared she'd lose her job. "They made me feel like *I* was the problem, like it was my fault. I started to believe it was."

So she kept silent. These are toxic secrets — the kind that gnaw at you over years, that over time make you feel less-than, that make you feel like no one will believe you or accept you, the kind that let you believe the lie that whatever happened must have been your fault. You can go on, live your life, and be a strong, self-sufficient woman — to the point where no one would really guess how isolating and exhausting it is to carry all that for so long. But the secrets are always there.

This is the tricky thing about shame, it weaves itself into everything. It makes itself at home in every moment, every memory, so that everything gets tainted with self-criticism and judgment. We forget how to be gentle with ourselves, how to forgive ourselves for what we couldn't have possibly known or fully understood or controlled given the resources we had at that time.

She wanted to be free. Through her work with the book, Aurora committed herself to the work of forgiveness — of others, but especially of herself. For too many years, she had confused responsibility and blame. She believed that if she took responsibility for mistakes she'd made, it meant that she had to live under their shadow forever. Shame had told her over and over, *Unless you're perfect, you don't deserve to be truly happy.* She thought about how long she'd carried that lie with her, and how it had affected her choices. Yes, she knew it — she wanted to be free.

While working through the book, she took a class at her church on forgiveness and was blessed with this liberating insight, "There is power in recognizing the wisdom that came from difficult and painful situations, how we encounter people for a reason and that we can grow from that." When we see that we were doing the best we could with the emotional and spiritual tools we had at the time, we can begin to acknowledge that we are as deserving of forgiveness as anyone. And as a person of faith, she frames it like this, "I know God loves me and has forgiven me. Why can't I believe that? I'm loved. I'm forgiven. I'm enough. I can give that to myself, too."

She realized, too, how the negative messages she'd replayed about herself were affecting her daughter's self-image. After all those years of saying she was unattractive and constantly putting herself down, she understood that she was unintentionally telling her daughter the same things. After all, people were always telling her daughter she looked just like her mother. So what message was she sending to her daughter when she said these horrible things about herself? Once she was able to find love for herself and her appearance, she saw the same spark within her daughter, that renewed confidence in herself. You never know what impressions you are making on others around you — which increases the importance of believing, speaking, and living love, with yourself and with others. My favorite thing about Aurora's journey that was such a profound moment to see, was the moment she looked at me with the sparkle in her eyes and finally said "*I AM* beautiful!

Like so many things in the human experience, it's not one-and-done. It's a practice. It's still work. She still has moments. But this is the important thing to remember, she now knows the way back to herself.

Day 31 Story: *Being imperfect is part of being human. It does not cut me off from being worthy of happiness, joy,* *and real connection. Shame does not get the final word. Love does!*

Your Turn!

- Can you identify moments, memories, or situations where you made choices that you have struggled to forgive yourself for?
- Have you kept silent or felt shame about something that happened to you that was beyond your control?
- What can Aurora's story offer as you contemplate embracing a new story about love and worthiness?

Signature yoga pose: *Warrior II.*

Why she loves it: *It always makes me feel strong no matter what kind of day I'm having, like I could do anything. It forces me to stand up straight and take notice of what type of woman I have become.*

What I see when she is in this pose: I see an amazing, strong, powerful woman who didn't realize how beautiful she was, inside and out. She was so used to being a warrior fighting for our country that she forgot to fight for herself. I couldn't be more proud of this woman and her beauty and her strength. She is a true warrior in all aspects of the word.

POSTSCRIPT

These stories are a sampling of the many journeys walked with *Pssst...Wanna Get Out of Your Own Way?* in the last couple of years. I am grateful to these participants for being so open, vulnerable, and brave with their stories.

It is in the sharing that we start to see that we're not alone. We start to see that our human experience is more similar than different, that we all long for many of the same things: freedom, connection, authentic self-love, real joy (the kind that lives deep down and isn't dependent on external things), peace, courage, the ability to make ourselves new when we realize we're stuck and unhappy.

These folks have shown that it's possible and have offered their personal insights into *how* to make it happen. My hope is that their work emboldens and inspires you to take those tentative first steps, even if you're unsure or skeptical or afraid.

If you're feeling ready to dive in, then let's go! You can get a copy of the book by visiting

http://www.amazon.com/author/JodieBaudek

In addition, we're up to tons of other good things that you can plug into. Check out these opportunities for connection and transformation:

- **Podcasts/Youtube**—Check out my weekly Podcasts & Youtube videos: "The Empowered Life with Jodie Baudek", and also, "Get Out Of Your Own Way with Dr Jim & Jodie" Be sure to subscribe to be the first to know of all updates!

- **Events**—Check back often at www.JodieBaudek.com & www.DrJimandJodie.com to get the latest info on speaking engagements, presentations, and seminars. Check out www.essenceol.com for Yoga & Pilates classes, workshops, and events.

As always, I welcome your questions and invite you into this Big Awesome Conversation we're all having together.

Printed in the United States
By Bookmasters